A Bill of Rights for Britain

CHATTO
Counter**Blasts**

Ronald
DWORKIN

A Bill of Rights
for Britain

Chatto & Windus
LONDON

Published in 1990 by
Chatto & Windus Ltd
20 Vauxhall Bridge Road
London SW1V 2SA

A CIP catalogue record for this book
is available from the British Library

ISBN 0 7011 3601 4

Photoset in Linotron Ehrhardt by
Rowland Phototypesetting Ltd
Bury St Edmunds, Suffolk
Printed in Great Britain by
St Edmundsbury Press Ltd
Bury St Edmunds, Suffolk

Liberty is Ill in Britain

GREAT BRITAIN was once a fortress for freedom. It claimed the great philosophers of liberty –
Milton and Locke and Paine and Mill. Its legal
tradition is irradiated with liberal ideas: that people
accused of crime are presumed to be innocent, that
no one owns another's conscience, that a man's
home is his castle. But now Britain offers less
formal legal protection to central freedoms than
most of its neighbours in Europe. I do not mean
that it has become a police state, of course. Citizens
are free openly to criticise the government, and the
government does not kidnap or torture or kill its
opponents. But liberty is nevertheless under threat
by a notable decline in the *culture* of liberty – the
community's shared sense that individual privacy
and dignity and freedom of speech and conscience
are crucially important and that they are worth
considerable sacrifices in official convenience or
public expense to protect.

The erosion of liberty is not the doing of only
one party or one government. Labour governments
in the 1970s compromised the rights of immigrants,
tried to stop publication of embarrassing political
material, and tolerated an outrageous censorship

and intimidation of journalists by the newspaper unions. But most of the worst examples of the attack on liberty have occurred in the last decade, and Margaret Thatcher and her government are more open in their indifference to liberty than their predecessors were.

Official Secrecy The list of liberties compromised or ignored in Britain in recent years is a long, sad one. Freedom of speech has consistently been sacrificed to liberty's most powerful enemy: official secrecy, the value rulers put on keeping their own acts and decisions dark. Censorship is no longer an isolated event accepted with great regret and keen sense of loss in the face of some emergency. On the contrary, censorship has become routine, an inexpensive way of the government's saving itself trouble or embarrassment.

Mrs Thatcher's government has indiscriminately prosecuted civil servants and others who revealed information they thought the public should know. It brought contempt proceedings against Harriet Harman for turning over to the press official records that had already been made public in open court, and prosecuted Clive Ponting for leaking records of no importance to security but which he believed showed grave official misconduct. A jury acquitted Ponting; and the government, furious, changed the Official Secrets Act to make it plain that the public interest could be no defence to any such charge in the future.

Publishing The government made Britain look ridiculous throughout the world when it tried every conceivable legal strategy to stop people reading *Spycatcher*, an unpleasant but harmless book about British security services, written by a former employee of Britain's secret service in defiance of his promise of confidentiality. Even after *Spycatcher* had been published in the United States, Australia and elsewhere, and Britons who travelled abroad had flooded the country with copies they brought back, the government still sought and won an injunction forbidding the *Sunday Times* and other papers from printing excerpts here, all the time conceding that publication posed not the slightest security risk. The government finally lost its preposterous battle, even in Britain, when the courts held that there was no sense in stopping the publication here of what was common knowledge in the rest of the world.

Broadcasting Censorship by intimidation has become sadly commonplace. Ministers now routinely denounce broadcasters as biased and unpatriotic. When Thames Television showed a film about the shooting of IRA members by British security officers in Gibraltar, called *Death on the Rock*, the Prime Minister and Home Secretary immediately

3

attacked the programme as deceptive and substantially untrue, though (as an eminent commission chaired by Lord Windlesham later concluded) it was neither.

Officials have no hesitation, moreover, in using direct censorship of television when they believe indirect methods will not work. It is incredible but true that under the Licence Agreement with the BBC, and under a Broadcasting Act regulating independent television, the Home Secretary has the power at any time to stop the broadcast of any matter or classes of matter he specifies. In 1988 he invoked that power in a massive way, to prohibit any broadcast of any interviews with representatives of various Northern Ireland organisations on any subject whatsoever, including the re-broadcast of films made decades ago. The order included not only the IRA but Sinn Fein, which is a legal party with a Member of Parliament. That was an uncommonly silly and pointless decision – the order allowed actors to read lines spoken by members of the forbidden organisations. It is also a direct and savage example of political censorship; it strikes to the heart of a journalist's right to speak and the public's right to hear.

The government recently suggested that it will change, in the broadcasting Bill scheduled shortly to become law, the standards that require television companies to maintain impartiality about matters of political controversy. Its proposed changes have not yet been announced, but since the government has widely criticised the media as being biased against it, many editors and journalists are now fearful of what will come.

Privacy and Surveillance Police wiretapping, bugging and secret surveillance are for all practical purposes legally uncontrolled in Britain, and the police have a quite scandalous power to invade the privacy of individuals. Under the Interception of Communications Act of 1985, the police can tap anyone's phone or read his mail if they have the permission not of a judge, as in other countries, but of a politician – the Home Secretary. (In what the statute describes as 'an urgent case', the Home Secretary himself need not even sign the order.)

The Act provides only an ineffective scheme of review of the Home Secretary's decisions. Different forms of review are conducted by a special tribunal of senior lawyers, who are appointed by the Prime Minister, and by a special Commissioner who is also appointed by the Prime Minister, and whose reports she can censor before publication. There are no effective sanctions against illegal wiretapping, and the Act expressly forbids the investigation, or even the *mention*, of wiretapping in court. Police use of bugging devices and secret video cameras is subject to no control at all, except Home Office guidelines and circulars which the police are free to ignore. All this would seem incredible in many other constitutional democracies.

Moralism Britain interferes much more with its citizen's private lives than it used to do, particularly about sex, which next to secrecy is the nation's chief obsession. The government's decision to implement Section 28 of the Local Government Act of 1988, which prohibits support for 'the teaching in any maintained school of the acceptability of homosexuality as a pretended family relationship', sent a chilling message of intolerance that is explicable only on nasty political grounds, whatever the legal consequences of that bizarre language turn out to be.

Protest Britain is less tolerant of political protest than many other nations, and much readier to deny that right for reasons only of convenience or distaste. Other countries wrestle with the difficult problem of allowing the maximum freedom of political protest consistent with public order and safety. In Britain freedom of protest is permitted only when the cost to public convenience is minimal. There is no general right to protest, and the use of even traditional public places for protest requires the prior approval of the police. The Campaign for Nuclear Disarmament, the Save Greece from Fascism, and the Northern Ireland Civil Rights Movement have all been denied the use of Trafalgar Square.

The 1986 Public Order Act requires advance notice even for peaceful processions or marches which cause no obstruction, and that Act makes the leader criminally responsible if the march takes a somewhat different route or starts later than the notice specified. The Act gives the police power to issue any order, at a public meeting of 20 or more persons, that they deem necessary to prevent 'serious disruption in the life of the community'. They can order a meeting or march to move or to reduce its numbers, for example, and the protest's leaders may be sent to jail if those orders are disobeyed. If protesters challenge the orders in court, the judge must uphold them if he decides that the police thought them necessary to maintain order, whether they actually were necessary or not. It is hard to imagine a scheme of regulating demonstrations in a democracy more mean-spirited to liberty, more contemptuous of the importance and value of committed protest.

Rights of Suspects British justice led the world in insisting on criminal procedures which provide strong protection against convicting innocent people. But under the pressure of terrorist threats these procedures are being abandoned, and the president of Britain's Law Society recently warned, at that group's annual conference, that the delicate balance between prosecution and defence was being upset in favour of the former. Parliament continues to re-enact the detention provisions of the Prevention of Terrorism Act, which allow people suspected of that crime to be held incommunicado for two days, and then for a further five days with the permission of the Home Secretary, without being charged with any crime or being allowed to see a lawyer in private. (Only 7 per cent of people detained in that way have ever been charged with any crime at all; the rest were released having, in effect, served a week's jail sentence by the fiat of a politician.) In 1988 the European Court of Human Rights declared these rules a violation of the European Convention of Human Rights, which Britain has signed, and ordered Britain to change them. The Thatcher government then argued that it had the right to derogate from its obligations under that Convention pursuant to Article 15, which allows a state to derogate in 'time of war or other public emergency'. The European Commission is now considering that claim.

Since the seventeenth century British law has insisted that in a criminal trial the State must prove the suspect's guilt by its own evidence and not out of his or her mouth. So the common law gave defendants a right of silence, and that right has been copied and respected in the jurisprudence of many other nations and in the famous Fifth Amendment to the United States Constitution. But the ancient right is about to be extinguished in the nation that invented it. In 1988 Mrs Thatcher's government announced that the principle would no longer hold in Northern Ireland, and might be curtailed in the rest of Britain soon. Under the Ulster rules, if a suspect refuses to answer questions put by the police that fact can count as evidence against him, even if the evidence was otherwise not sufficient to convict. If he refuses to testify at trial, the judge or jury is entitled to draw an inference of guilt. That is exactly what Senator Joe McCarthy proposed when he attacked the Fifth Amendment in the United States in the 1950s. The Supreme Court protected the ancient right of silence there, but no British court can now prevent it from being annihilated here.

The Tyranny of Convenience

THE TORY government calls itself conservative, but it is wrecking the best part of Britain's legal heritage. Thatcher's people are not despots. But they have a more mundane and corrupting insensitivity to liberty. Of course any democratic government must balance the interests and demands of different sections of the public and choose policies they think best for the community as a whole. It must therefore restrain people's freedom in various ways. It must lay down rules regulating how fast or in what direction people may drive, the size and character of the buildings they may build, the terms on which they may hire or fire employees, when and how they may merge or combine their businesses, and thousands of other matters.

In a culture of liberty, however, the public shares a sense, almost as a matter of secular religion, that certain freedoms are in principle exempt from this ordinary process of balancing and regulation. It insists that government may not dictate its citizens' convictions or tastes, or decide what they say or hear or read or write, or deny them a fair trial by historical standards, even when it believes, with however good reason, that infringing these liberties would on balance protect security or promote economy or efficiency or convenience. In a culture of liberty, these freedoms cannot be abridged except to prevent a clear and serious danger – a calamity – and even then only so far as is absolutely necessary to prevent it.

Of course difficult questions arise about exactly which activities should belong to the protected system of liberties, about how clear and present a particular danger is, and about when less stringent means of regulation than censorship or prohibition are available. People equally committed to freedom disagree about whether, for example, the dangers of tobacco advertising or the offensiveness of racial epithets justify withholding protection from these forms of speech. The essence of liberty is not agreement over particular hard cases, however, but an attitude: that the traditional liberties are so crucial to human dignity that hard questions should be decided in their favour as far as possible, that a fence should be constructed around and at some distance from the heartland of free expression, privacy and fair criminal process, that government should bear the onus of demonstrating that *any* interference with *any* part of the fundamental liberties is really necessary to secure some essential goal.

That is the spirit in which a culture of liberty approaches hard questions about speech and protest and the right to silence and the rights of minorities. It does not ask whether the public will be more or less pleased, on the whole, if there is less sex on television. Or whether the loss of valuable information to the public will outbalance the gain to the security system if television programmes about Gibraltar or Northern Ireland are censored, or whether government operates more smoothly and efficiently when public officials are prosecuted for leaking embarrassing information, or whether there will be less crime if suspects are henceforth denied the right of silence.

These questions are unfair to liberty, because the value of liberty cannot be measured piecemeal, in iotas of information sacrificed or imagination stifled or creativity impaired or innocent people convicted. Measured case-by-case against the immediate aims of ordinary politics, the value of liberty will always seem speculative and marginal; it will always seem academic, abstract, and dispensable. Liberty is already lost, whatever the outcome, as soon as old freedoms are put at risk in cost-benefit politics. A decent nation is committed to freedom in a different way. It knows that liberty's value lies on a different scale, that invading freedom is not a useful technique of government but a compromise of the nation's dignity and civilisation.

The present government rejects that view of liberty's value. It makes freedom just another commodity, to be enjoyed when there is no particular political or commercial or administrative price to be paid for it, but abandoned, with no evident grief, when the price begins to rise. That is not despotism. But it cheapens liberty and diminishes the nation.

The European Convention of Human Rights

WHEN THE eminent French historian François Furet came recently to Britain to lecture on the occasion of the bicentennial of the French Revolution, he said that the signal triumph of democracy in our time is the growing acceptance and enforcement of a crucial idea: that democracy is not the same thing as majority rule, and that in a real democracy liberty and minorities have legal protection in the form of a written constitution that even Parliament cannot change to suit its whim or policy. Under that vision of democracy, a bill of individual constitutional rights is part of fundamental law, and judges, who are not elected and who are therefore removed from the pressures of partisan politics, are responsible for interpreting and enforcing that Bill of Rights as they are for all other parts of the legal system.

The United States was born committed to that idea of democracy, and now every member of the European Community but Britain accepts it, and so do the great majority of other mature democracies, including India, Canada, and almost all the other democratic Commonwealth nations. Britain stands alone in insisting that Parliament must have absolutely unlimited legal power to do anything it wishes.

British constitutional lawyers once bragged that a constitutional Bill of Rights was unnecessary because in Britain the people can trust the rulers they elect. But now a great many people – more than ever before – believe that this is no longer true, and that the time has come for Britain to join other democracies and put its Parliament under law. Charter 88, an organisation created to press that argument, has attracted impressive support at every level of British society. Would a charter of constitutional rights help to restore the British culture of liberty? Learned Hand, a great American constitutional judge, said that when the spirit of freedom dies in a people, no constitution or Supreme Court can bring it back to life. And it is true that many nations with formal constitutional guarantees, including some of the European nations that have made the European Convention of Human Rights part of their own law, fail fully to honour their constitutional rights in practice. But though a written constitution is certainly not a sufficient condition for liberty to thrive again in Britain, it may well be a necessary one.

Of course the idea of a Bill of Rights is rejected by many of the people you might expect to reject it: the leading politicians of both of the two great parties whose power, when in office, would be curtailed if people enjoyed constitutional rights as individuals. Most Tory politicians, in spite of the shambles they have made of liberty in recent years, think that their government is too much rather than too little hedged in by judges. They howl whenever judges find the actions of ministers and officials illegal, as judges have done several times in recent years, and they call for Parliament to change the law to keep the judges off their backs. The Labour Party, too, has so far been adamantly opposed to a constitutional Bill of Rights, in spite of its own historical concern for individual liberty. Fortunately, there are now indications that Labour has changed its mind and will support a Bill of Rights. But most of the pressure has come from the bottom rather than the top, from people demanding the rights and liberties that in other countries belong to them, not to the politicians.

How could a Bill of Rights be enacted? One way would be remarkably simple. As I said earlier, Britain is already committed by international treaty to a charter of constitutional rights called the European Convention. With very little procedural fuss Parliament could enact a statute providing that the principles of that convention are henceforth part of the law of Britain, enforceable by British judges in British courts. A statute to that effect has been introduced in Parliament on three occasions in recent years; it was actually debated, as a private member's Bill, in 1986, though it did not obtain the necessary majority for closure to permit a vote.

The European Convention was adopted in 1950, when the memory of Fascist tyranny was fresh, and it has now been signed by all the nations of western Europe. Under the treaty, an individual citizen in each of the member countries has the right, when he or she thinks his nation has broken some covenant of the Convention, to bring a complaint before the European Commission. If the Commission decides that the individual has satisfied procedural requirements, and that his complaint is not manifestly ill-founded, it begins an investigation and at the same time attempts a friendly settlement between the individual and his or her government. If no friendly settlement is reached, and the Commission decides that a violation has occurred, it may assign the matter to the judges of the European Court of Human Rights in Strasbourg, and if that Court agrees that the Convention has been violated, it orders the offending nation to change its laws to bring them into accord with what the Convention requires.

Britain has been a frequent defendant before the European Court, as one would expect, given its recent insensitivity to individual freedom. Since 1965 twice as many petitions have been lodged against it as against any other member, and it has lost more serious cases than any other nation. The Court has ordered Britain to stop inhuman and degrading treatment of suspected terrorists, to allow prisoners access to a lawyer while in jail, to stop birching as a punishment in the Isle of Man and caning as a punishment in State schools, to repeal certain laws against homosexuality in Northern Ireland, to end the worst forms of discrimination in immigration, to improve the legal rights of prisoners and mental patients, and to adopt protection against indiscriminate wiretapping and covert surveillance. (It is doubtful whether the government's response to the last of these orders – the Interception of Communications Act I described earlier – actually satisfied the Court's decree, and the matter will presumably be argued before the Court again.)

When the European Commission decided that Harriet Harman had an admissible case before the European Court, the Thatcher government quickly settled the case, paid her legal costs, and amended the law. The European Court had already declared, in 1976, that the conviction of the *Sunday Times* for contempt of court, because it had published information about the never-ending Thalidomide litigation while the case was technically still pending, violated the Convention, and the Contempt of

Court Act of 1981 was enacted in response to the Court's decree. In 1988, as I said, the European Court ordered Britain to cease detaining prisoners for a week without any judicial warrant. The Commission recently ruled that the *Sunday Times*, the *Observer* and the *Guardian* have made out a case, appropriate for the Commission to consider further, that the preliminary injunction against publishing *Spycatcher* excerpts violated the Convention. Other Strasbourg proceedings against the United Kingdom are pending.

In theory, then, Britain already has a constitution of individual rights, enforceable by a court in Strasbourg, which Parliament is powerless to abridge except in a case of emergency. But the European Convention is no substitute for a domestic Bill of Rights interpreted and enforced by British judges trained in British traditions. A private citizen who feels his rights under the Convention have been violated must first exhaust whatever remedies might be thought to be available at home, and then prepare and argue a case first before the European Commission and then, if matters go that far, before the European Court. The process is fearsomely expensive (there is, for all practical purposes, no legal aid available) and takes on average six years, by which time, particularly in cases involving censorship, the issue is almost always academic.

Two thirds of European countries, including all

the other major ones, have made the Convention part of their domestic law, so that it can be raised and its benefit claimed in national courts. But Britain has not done so. Some British judges believe that they nevertheless have the power, and indeed the responsibility, to take the principles of the Convention into account in interpreting British law. Several judges in the *Spycatcher* litigation, for example, said that when British law is unclear, it should be read so as to be consistent with Article 10 of the Convention, which declares that a member nation may not abridge free speech, except as is 'necessary in a democratic society'. Some judges go further, and accept a general presumption that Parliament does not intend to violate the Convention, or to permit ministers to do so, unless the plain language of some statute indicates otherwise, and that ministers must therefore exercise the general powers granted by statutes only in ways the Convention permits.

Many senior judges have been unwilling to apply any such presumption, however, even in cases in which it would be natural to do so. The Court of Appeal recently upheld the Home Secretary's ban against interviews with Sinn Fein and other organisations; it declined to assume that Parliament did not intend him to have power to violate Article 10 of the Convention. The Master of the Rolls, Lord Donaldson, said that that presumption amounts to bringing the Convention into British law by the back door when Parliament has conspicuously declined to bring it in by the front, by explicitly incorporating it.

But of course even judges who are ready to give effect to the Convention by way of a presumption about parliamentary intent cannot do so when a statute or the common law is not vague or ambiguous but expressly requires what the Convention prohibits. The Prevention of Terrorism Act, which allows suspects to be held for a week without being charged, is not unclear. Nor is the Public Order Act which gives the police such unjustified control over protest marches. If Parliament abolishes the right of silence in Britain as a whole, its draftsmen will make plain that that is what is intended. Judges have no power to protect the people from such statutes, even if the judges think the statutes are plain violations of Britain's international obligations under the European Convention.

If Parliament made the European Convention part of British law, on the other hand, judges could decide on their own whether some official action or parliamentary statute violated the Convention. They could decide that question in the same way they decide any other issue of law. So the broadcasting ban, and all the other tawdry acts of censorship that violate Britain's solemn obligations under the treaty, could be challenged at once and not five or six years later when the government's aim of stopping public access to information has long since been achieved anyway. Official denials of privacy, or of the right of legitimate protest, or of the rights of people accused of crimes, could be challenged at once, and not years later when the damage was done and long past undoing.

If the judges used this new authority well, the most important and immediate benefit would be a revitalisation of the liberty and dignity of the people. Government and officials would no longer be so free to keep secrets from the people they are supposed to serve, or to ignore rights the nation has a solemn obligation to respect. Other, more speculative but in the long run equally important, benefits might then follow.

The European Convention speaks in abstract terms, and subjects many of the rights it declares to equally abstract exceptions. Article 8, for example, which declares that everyone has the right to respect for his private and family life, home and correspondence, allows an exception for measures 'necessary in a democratic society in the interests of national security, public safety or the economic well-being of the country', or 'necessary for the protection of health and morals'. Different lawyers take different views about what such phrases mean. British judges could not adopt a *less* generous interpretation of these abstract clauses than the Strasbourg Court has established in its own decisions; a British court could not deny rights the Strasbourg Court had recognised. But British judges could certainly adopt, for Britain, a *more* generous interpretation, using the rich and special traditions of the British common law to develop out of the Convention a particularly British view of the fundamental rights of citizens in a democratic society. They might decide, for example, that Article 6 of the Convention, which requires 'fair' criminal trials, should be interpreted to require nations to observe guarantees established in their own legal traditions, which in the case of Britain would include the right to silence.

If British judges began to create as well as follow constitutional jurisprudence in that way, their decisions would be bound to influence the Commission and Court in Strasbourg, as well as the courts of the other nations who have signed the Convention, and, indeed, of all the other nations across the globe who are now wrestling with the problem of making abstract human rights concrete. Incorporation would put the special skills of British lawyers and judges, and the heritage of British legal principle, at the service of the civilised world. Britain could become once again a leader in defining and protecting individual freedom, instead of a sullen defendant giving ground to liberty only when ordered to do so by a foreign court.

Law and lawyers might then begin to play a different, more valuable role in society than they now even aim to have. The courts, charged with the responsibility of creating from the Convention a distinctly British scheme of human rights and liberty, might think more in terms of principle and less in terms of narrow precedent. University law courses and faculties might develop in the same direction, trying to produce a legal profession that could be the conscience, not just the servant, of government and industry. Different men and women might then be tempted to the law as a career, and from their ranks a more committed and idealistic generation of judges might emerge, encouraging a further cycle in the renaissance of liberty. No part of this attractive chain reaction would be inevitable, of course, even if Britain did decide in some way to incorporate the European Convention into its domestic law. But it is hard to imagine a political decision more likely to set it off.

How Could the Convention be Incorporated?

THE EUROPEAN Convention is not a perfect Bill of Rights for Britain. It was a compromise drafted to accommodate a variety of nations with different legal systems and traditions; it is in many ways weaker than the American Bill of Rights; and it is hedged about with vague limitations and powerful escape clauses of different sorts. The Convention does protect liberty better than it is now protected by Parliament alone, however, as recent history shows. It protects freedom of speech, religion and expression, privacy, and the most fundamental rights of accused criminals, and it grants in an indirect but effective way rights against discrimination. Since Britain is already subject to the Convention as a matter of both moral obligation and international law, it would plainly be easier to enact that charter into British law, substantially as it is, perhaps with clarifying changes and additions from other international covenants Britain has also signed, than to begin drafting and debating a wholly new Bill of Rights. Even if it were possible to adopt an entirely new set of rights, perhaps modelled on the American Constitution, the European Convention would remain law enforceable in Strasbourg, and the potential conflict between the two fundamental charters of rights would be a source of wasteful confusion.

So those who love liberty should unite in supporting the incorporation of the Convention. But how can this be done, and in what form should it be done? Suppose Parliament declared tomorrow that both its own past and future statutes and the acts of ministers and officials under them shall be null and void unless they are in conformity with the Convention's principles. Would not a future Parliament, tired of that constraint, have the power simply to repeal the incorporation? Indeed, would it not repeal the incorporation automatically whenever it enacted a statute inconsistent with the Convention, in which case incorporation would be a nonsense from the start? Suppose Parliament tomorrow both incorporated the Convention *and* provided that the incorporation could not be repealed by a future Parliament except by an extraordinary majority of, say, three-quarters of the members. Could not a future Parliament, by ordinary majority vote, simply repeal the provision requiring an extraordinary majority?

Many lawyers assume that it could. So does Roy

Hattersley, the Deputy Leader of the Labour Party; he defends his opposition to a Bill of Rights on the ground, among others, that even if Parliament incorporated the European Convention unanimously, a future Parliament could simply repeal the incorporation any time it proved inconvenient. (Hattersley himself has recently proposed, however, that a new second chamber of Parliament be elected, to replace the present House of Lords, which would have power to delay any legislation limiting specified rights for the life of the Parliament in which such legislation is introduced. This proposal assumes that Parliament *can* change constitutional rules in a way that it cannot then revoke under the old rules it decided to change. If Parliament can irreversibly limit its own power by creating a new chamber with new powers of delay, why can it not irreversibly limit its own power by incorporating a constitutional Bill of Rights?)

In any case, I disagree with the judgment of law that Parliament cannot limit the power of a future Parliament. That judgment assumes that any Parliament has the legal power to do absolutely anything it wishes to do, notwithstanding what earlier Parliaments have done. What is the authority for that proposition? It plainly does not owe *its* authority to any parliamentary decision, because it would beg the question for Parliament to decide that its own power was unlimited.

British lawyers say that Parliament is an absolute sovereign because that seems (for most of them intuitively and unreflectively) the best interpretation of British legal history, practice and tradition. But legal history and practice can change with great speed. Suppose a national debate on constitutional principle took place, after which Parliament declared that the European Convention was incorporated into British law, and also declared that this decision could itself be repealed or amended only by a special procedure requiring an extraordinary majority of both Houses. Then British constitutional history would have been altered just by that decision having been made, understood and accepted by the public as a whole. Practice and tradition would have changed, and the old interpretation, which declares absolute parliamentary supremacy, would plainly no longer fit. Judges would have no legal or logical reason not to hold future Parliaments to the decision the nation had made. They would have no legal or logical reason not to insist that only an extraordinary majority could restore the present situation.

So the popular argument that there is no way Parliament can impose a constitutional Bill of Rights on a later Parliament is at least dubious. But notice that I have so far been discussing what might be called a *strong* form of incorporation, which provides that any statute inconsistent with the Convention is null and void. Several influential supporters of a Bill of Rights (including Lord Scarman, a former member of the House of Lords, who has been a pioneer in the argument for incorporation) have proposed that in the first instance incorporation should take what is technically a weaker form: the incorporating statute should provide that an inconsistent statute is null and void unless Parliament has expressly stated that it *intends* the statute to override the Convention. In practice this technically weaker version of incorporation would probably provide almost as much protection as the stronger one. If a government conceded that its statute violated the Convention, it would have no defence before the Commission or Court in Strasbourg. In any case, quite apart from that practical point, no respectable government would wish to announce that it did not care whether its legislation or decisions violated the country's domestic promises and international obligations. If a government felt itself able to make such an announcement, except in the most extraordinary circumstances, the spirit of liberty would be dead anyway, beyond the power of any constitution to revive.

At least in the first instance, therefore, proponents should press for the weaker version of incorporation. If they succeed, then unless Parliament has expressly provided to the contrary any citizen will have the right in British courts to challenge a law or an official decision on the ground that it is offensive to the Convention's principles. Some European nations have established special courts to hear constitutional challenges. But it would be better, at least in Britain, to allow any division of the High Court to entertain such a challenge. Constitutional issues are not so arcane or specialised that ordinary judges, assisted by counsel in the normal way, could not master them.

Should Parliament be Supreme?

THAT IS the case for incorporating the European Convention into domestic British law. It is no mystery that powerful politicians are reluctant to accept that case. Ministers and officials are rarely keen to justify themselves before judges, and constitutional rights often make important political objectives more difficult to achieve. These are the costs of a culture of liberty, and politicians, above all, hate to pay them. What is surprising, however, is the ineptness of the arguments politicians have deployed against incorporation. In the rest of this essay, I shall consider all the arguments of which I am aware.

The politicians say that the very idea of a Bill of Rights restricting the power of Parliament is hostile to the British tradition that Parliament and Parliament alone should be sovereign. That supposed tradition seems less appealing now, when a very powerful executive and well-disciplined political parties mean less effective power for backbench MPs than it did before these developments. The tradition has already been compromised in recent decades, moreover. It was altered by the European Communities Act, for example, under which judges have the power to override parliamentary decisions in order to enforce directly effective Community rules.

In any case, quite apart from these considerations, incorporating the European Convention would not diminish Parliament's present power in any way that could reasonably be thought objectionable. Parliament is *already* bound by international law to observe the terms of that Convention. If the Convention were incorporated in what I have called the strong form, under which a future Parliament would not have the legal power to violate the Convention even if it expressly said it intended to do so, then the power of Parliament might be somewhat more limited than it is now, because British judges might develop a special British interpretation of the Convention that in some cases recognised individual constitutional rights the Strasbourg Court would not.

It is hard to argue that this further limitation would be wrong in principle, however. Britain agreed when it accepted the European Convention and the jurisdiction of the European Court of Human Rights, that it would be bound by the principles laid down in the Convention as these principles were interpreted not by Parliament but by a group of judges. If that limitation on the power of Parliament is acceptable, how can it be unacceptable that the principles be interpreted not by mainly foreign judges but by British judges trained in the common law and in the legal and political traditions of their own country?

The argument for parliamentary supremacy would be irrelevant, moreover, if the Convention were incorporated in the weaker form I suggested should be the initial goal. For then Parliament could override the Convention by mere majority vote, provided it was willing expressly to concede its indifference about doing so. No doubt that condition would, in practice, prevent a government from introducing legislation it might otherwise enact. That is the point of incorporation, even in the weak form. But forcing Parliament to make the choice between obeying its international obligations and admitting that it is violating them does not limit

Parliament's supremacy, but only its capacity for duplicity. Candour is hardly inconsistent with sovereignty.

Is Incorporation Undemocratic?

THE ARGUMENT for parliamentary supremacy is often thought to rest on a more important and fundamental argument, however, according to which Britain should not have subscribed to the European Convention in the first place. This is the argument: that it is undemocratic for appointed judges rather than an elected Parliament to have the last word about what the law is. People who take that view will resist incorporation, because incorporation enlarges the practical consequences of what they regard as the mistake of accepting the Convention. They will certainly resist the idea that domestic judges should have the power to read the Convention more liberally and so provide more protection than Strasbourg requires.

Their argument misunderstands what democracy is, however. In the first place, it confuses democracy with the power of elected officials. There is no genuine democracy, even though officials have been elected in otherwise fair elections, unless voters have had access to the information they need so that their votes can be knowledgeable choices rather than only manipulated responses to advertising campaigns. Citizens of a democracy must be able to participate in government not just spasmodically, in elections from time to time, but constantly through informed and free debate about their government's performance between elections. Those evident requirements suggest what other nations have long ago realised: that Parliament *must* be constrained in certain ways in order that democracy be genuine rather than sham. The argument that a Bill of Rights would be undemocratic is therefore not just wrong but the opposite of the truth.

The depressing story of the Thatcher government's concentrated assault on free speech is more than enough to prove that point. In the Harman, Ponting and *Spycatcher* cases, in denying a public interest exception in the new Official Secrets Act, in the broadcasting bans, in the *Death on the Rock* matter, government tried to censor information of the type citizens need in order to vote intelligently or criticise officials effectively. The officials who took these decisions acted out of various motives: out of concern for confidentiality, or to discourage

33

views they thought dangerous, or to improve the morale of the police and security services, or sometimes just to protect themselves from political damage. But none of these reasons is good enough: <u>in a democracy officials have no right to dictate what the voters should know or think</u>. The politicians would very likely have acted differently in every one of these cases if Article 10 of the European Convention had been part of British law, and the prospect of judicial intervention had been immediate and certain rather than delayed and in doubt. British democracy would obviously have been strengthened not weakened as a result.

It is true, however, that the European Convention forbids governments to adopt or retain some laws that a majority of their citizens do want, and would continue to want even if they had all the information anyone might wish. The European Court struck down Northern Ireland's homosexuality law, for example, not because the Court doubted that a majority of the voters of Northern Ireland wanted that law, but because the Convention prohibits that form of discrimination whether the majority wishes it or not. If the European Convention were incorporated, British judges might strike down Britain's blasphemy law, which prohibits books or art deeply offensive to orthodox Christianity, even if a majority favoured retaining that law. The blasphemy law violates Articles 9 and 10 of the Convention, which protect freedom of conscience and free speech. In my view (although British courts have rejected the suggestion) the blasphemy law also violates Articles 9 and 14, which taken together prohibit religious discrimination, because that law discriminates in favour of Christianity. (Moslems said it was unjust that Salman Rushdie's book, *The Satanic Verses*, could not be prosecuted as blasphemous of their religion.) Of course the blasphemy law should not be extended to other religions, as they argued it should. It should instead be repealed, because it would violate the Convention even if it applied to religion in general.

Would it offend democracy if a British court had the power to strike down the blasphemy law as inconsistent with the Convention? No, because true democracy is not just *statistical* democracy, in which anything a majority or plurality wants is legitimate for that reason, but *communal* democracy, in which majority decision is legitimate only if it is a majority within a community of equals. That means not only that everyone must be allowed to participate in politics as an equal, through the vote and through freedom of speech and protest, but that political decisions must treat everyone with equal concern and respect, that each individual person must be guaranteed fundamental civil and political rights no combination of other citizens can take away, no matter how numerous they are or how much they despise his or her race or morals or way of life.

That view of what democracy means is at the heart of all the charters of human rights, including the European Convention. It is now the settled concept of democracy in Europe, the mature, principled concept that has now triumphed throughout Western Europe as well as in North America. It dominates the powerful movement towards democracy in Eastern Europe and Russia, and it was suppressed only with the most horrible tyranny in China. The rival, pure statistical concept of democracy, according to which democracy is consistent with oppressing minorities, was the concept proclaimed as justification by the Communist tyrannies after the Second World War: they said democracy meant government in the interests of the masses. The civilised world has recoiled from the totalitarian view, and it would be an appalling irony if Britain now embraced it as a reason for denying minorities constitutional rights.

This seems to me a decisive answer to the argument that incorporation would be undemocratic. I hope and believe that a different but equally decisive answer can also be made in Britain now: that the argument is self-defeating because the great majority of British people themselves rejects the crude statistical view of democracy on which the argument is based. Even people who do not think of themselves as belonging to any minority have good reasons for insisting that a majority's power to rule should be limited. Something crucially important to them – their religious freedom or professional independence or liberty of conscience, for example – might one day prove inconvenient to the government of the day. Even people who cannot imagine being isolated in that way might prefer to live in a genuine political community, in which everyone's dignity as an equal is protected, rather than just in a state they control.

That attractive impulse lies dormant in day-to-day political argument about how to fight terrorism or whether tolerance for homosexuals should be promoted with taxpayers' money or when suspected criminals' telephones should be tapped. But it might well surface during a general constitutional debate, when the nation reflects about its traditions and its image of itself. A public opinion poll in Britain in 1986, taken before a parliamentary debate about incorporation, reported that twice as many of those questioned favoured incorporation as opposed it, and that 71 per cent thought a constitutional Bill of Rights would improve democracy. Such polls are unreliable in various ways, but the dramatic preference for incorporation is nevertheless impressive. Britain will not have a Bill of Rights, even in the relatively weak form we have been discussing, unless it turns out, after an intense period of public

37

debate, that the preference is genuine, that the British people do share a constitutional sense of justice. If so, and if we assume that this sense of justice will be shared by their descendants, then the argument that incorporation is undemocratic will have been defeated on its own terms.

Is Incorporation Unnecessary?

ROY HATTERSLEY recently proposed that Parliament undertake a programme of comprehensive legislation that would, among other things, create a freedom of information Act, expand legal aid provision, and provide better remedies against discrimination. He proposes this desirable package, however, not in addition to incorporating the European Convention, as one might expect, but as an alternative, as if a constitutional Bill of Rights would be unnecessary if the legislation he described were adopted.

Of course Parliament should enact such legislation, whether or not it decides to incorporate the Convention, and the sooner the better. Hattersley's

charter of rights would implement some of the
Convention's requirements. It would also add pro-
tections, like strong freedom of information procedures that allow citizens to obtain official
documents, for example, that the Convention,
which sets minimum standards not upper limits,
does not itself require. It would be a serious mistake, however, to think that such legislation would
be an effective substitute for incorporation. Hattersley's proposals are limited to certain selected
improvements; they would not protect individual
liberty anywhere near as broadly as the Convention
does. Nothing in Hattersley's proposals suggests a
general right to freedom of expression, of the kind
that would protect journalists from trades union
censorship, for example; and many other rights
protected by the Convention, including rights to
compensation if a future Labour government
should renationalise privatised industries, have no
place in his proposed charter. I do not mean that
Hattersley's proposals are unfairly partisan. Any
detailed list of rights a particular party or government drafts for ordinary legislation will reflect its
own special concerns. It cannot provide the same
broad protection of individual freedom, or inspire
the same public sense in the impartiality of basic
rights, as a general convention of human rights can,
particularly a convention that has been adopted by
all the nations of Europe and interpreted by diverse

and independent judges, both international and domestic.

Hattersley's list of rights to be established by legislation could be repealed, moreover, by ordinary legislation whenever a later government found some restriction inconvenient. He also proposes, it is true, a major constitutional restructuring that he suggests would protect his charter of rights from future change. He proposes to replace the House of Lords with a second legislative chamber, elected by regions rather than on one-person-one-vote principles and therefore likely to be dominated by the Labour party, and he proposes that that second chamber should have the power to delay any repeal of any part of the charter of rights for the life of a Parliament. That seems an improbable constitutional development. In any case, an elected second chamber, whichever political party controlled it, would be a poor vehicle for protecting liberty from politicians tempted to sacrifice it to other goals, or for keeping individuals or unpopular minorities safe from the prejudice or indifference of majority will.

Will the Judges Have to Work Too Hard?

THE REMAINING objections I shall consider appeal not to philosophical principles about parliamentary supremacy or democracy or the superiority of ordinary legislation, but to more practical problems associated with the British judicial system. I begin with the most surprising of these. It is said that British judges are already overworked, and that asking them to consider constitutional questions as well as the ordinary legal claims they now entertain would impose far too great a burden on them. Judges themselves, I fear, make that argument: in a recent television discussion every judge who spoke against the proposal (some spoke for it) gave that as his reason. But the fear of overwork is surely exaggerated. Canadian judges complained of overwork when the Canadian Charter of Human Rights was first adopted, but most of them now concede that the additional work is becoming manageable.

I do not doubt that if the Convention did become part of British internal law, enterprising lawyers would make constitutional claims in a wide variety of criminal and even civil proceedings. It would cost their clients little for them to add, to any other claim or defence they make, that the police used unconscionable methods forbidden by Article 6 of the Convention, that the punishment threatened is inhuman or degrading and so contrary to Article 3, that the statute in question in some way curtails freedom of expression contrary to Article 10 or infringes privacy contrary to Article 8, or some other charge under some other article.

Judges would, of course, have to consider any such claim. But they would soon gain enough experience in constitutional matters quickly to see which of such claims had no merit. The decisions of the Strasbourg Court would be available, and British precedents would soon begin to build up, in the normal common law manner. Judges have a variety of traditional techniques for disposing of frivolous arguments in a way that makes counsel less likely to repeat them, moreover, and foolish litigation is discouraged by the normal practice that the loser must pay the winner's costs.

But suppose the fear of judicial overwork were well-founded. Suppose that even after plainly un-meritorious claims had been weeded out, constitutional issues took up so much judicial time that the overall legal system did suffer from clogging and lack of time for other matters. That would mean that the situation of freedom and justice in Britain is even worse than advocates of a Bill of Rights fear. It would then be preposterous to complain that it would have been better to save judges the work than to ask them to help defend the fundamental rights of British citizens. The appropriate solution – the only defensible solution – would then be to strengthen the judiciary.

If nothing else worked, then more judges could be appointed – there is no lack of qualified senior lawyers. But it is far from clear that new judges would be required. The British judicial system is famously under-financed and inefficient: even the most senior judges are given next to no secretarial, library or other assistance. In America every judge in the federal system, and almost every judge in the higher state courts, is assisted by at least one full-time paid clerk, and justices of the Supreme Court, which has the greatest burden of constitutional cases, each have exclusive use of four clerks.

Law clerks are generally recent and distinguished graduates of law schools, who serve as clerks for one or two years before beginning their own professional or academic careers. They are fresh from a more intense study of constitutional issues in law school than most judges have time to pursue on their own. Several British judges who are familiar with the American practice are already anxious to

43

move some way towards it, and would be particularly ready to do so if their work were expanded by incorporating the European Convention into British law.

The cost would be minimal, and the benefits in judicial imagination, improved training of the lawyers who became law clerks, and improved connections between the academic legal world and the bench would be significant, quite apart from the value of the practice in assisting judges asked to undertake a new department of work. Any problem of judicial overload could therefore be cured if the government were to spend more money on justice, by appointing new judges or allowing the present judges to use their time better. So the argument that incorporation would overwork the judges is actually an argument based on stinginess, a particularly debased form of the bad idea that rights should be denied when it is expensive or otherwise inconvenient to recognise them.

Are the Judges Up to the Job?

IF EVEN the weak version of incorporating the European Convention were adopted, judges would have more power than they do now. The additional power would be a matter of degree rather than of kind, because, as I said, some judges already appeal to the Convention as an aid to interpreting the will of Parliament, and because under the weak version of incorporation Parliament would have ultimate power to oust the jurisdiction of the judges, if it were willing to declare its intention not to respect the Convention. But the increase in the judges' role would be significant even if only quantitative, and that provokes an objection which is thought particularly powerful on the left of British politics.

It claims that British judges are, as a group, drawn from a very narrow and privileged section of the community, that they are insensitive or hostile to the interests and convictions of the rest of the nation, that they have for generations shown a collective bias for property and the middle class and against the trades-union movement, and that they

45

therefore cannot be trusted with the increased political power that incorporation, even in a weak form, would give them. This view of British judges is, in my view, both exaggerated and dated, but it does have a foundation in truth. Judges are drawn from the bar, which remains an élitist profession, and an unconscionably high percentage of them are Oxbridge graduates.

Compared to the American federal judges appointed before the Reagan administration, many judges in this country do seem conservative in their approach to civil rights, and often strike American lawyers as jurisprudentially unsophisticated and in the grip of antique views of precedent and statutory interpretation. But there have been remarkable exceptions, and the trend seems to be moving in the other direction. In different decisions in recent cases, Mr Justices Hoffman and Scott, the Vice-Chancellor Sir Nicholas Brown-Wilkinson, Lord Justices Bingham, Taylor and Woolf, and Lords Bridge, Oliver and Templeman, just as a few random examples, have offered arguments sensitive to liberty and fully mindful of judicial responsibilities in a democracy. In certain areas, moreover, British judges have proved imaginative and adventurous: they have recently developed, on their own, quite remarkable procedures of judicial review of administrative decisions, for example.

In any case the argument that British judges

cannot be trusted with constitutional rights makes an obviously untenable assumption: that judges will remain the same kind of people, and decide cases in the same kinds of way, whether or not they are asked to enforce a Bill of constitutional rights. If the Convention were incorporated into British law, even the most legally conservative judges would believe themselves bound to apply that decision in the spirit in which it was taken; in any case they would know they were obliged, by the act of incorporation, to have regard to decisions of the European Court. The legal culture would have changed around them: legal education and professional literature and debate would be based on new assumptions. In time, as I said earlier, the character of the bar and then the bench might well change in consequence. If the experiment worked, different men and women from different backgrounds would want to be lawyers, and these would include many who were attracted to law as an instrument of social justice. They would be trained differently, in a more international and cosmopolitan style, taught by a law faculty engaged in a different kind of research. Judges would soon begin to be drawn from a very different and much more diverse and exciting profession.

Suppose all this is wrong, however, and too many judges continue to be insensitive to the values of liberty and equality. How much would have been lost by incorporation then? Some writers suppose that bad judges armed with a Bill of Rights can wreck the nation. It is closer to the truth to say that they can merely disappoint it, as the Supreme Court now dominated by Reagan's ultra-conservative appointments is disappointing America. Conservative or unimaginative judges who refused to exercise their power to check ministers and officials or to set aside Parliamentary statutes would simply be leaving the legal world as it would have been *without* incorporation. At worst nothing substantial would have been lost, and it is extremely unlikely that nothing would have been gained. Some judges would exercise their new power well even if most did not, and the profession and the public would have a new basis for criticising and educating the laggards. Litigants who were denied their rights in decisions the profession criticised would be more likely to appeal to Strasbourg, and the European Court would hand down decisions that even the most conservative judges would then be obliged to follow in future cases.

It is odd how often all this is misunderstood. Lawyers hostile to incorporation warn that it would be unwise to trust a constitutional guarantee of free speech to British judges, who in the past have shown themselves insensitive to that right. But even if the judges did no more to protect speech under a clear constitutional direction than they did without it, which is implausible, the situation would not be worse than if they had not been directed at all. Other lawyers point to the fact that the American Supreme Court did not prevent the American government from interning citizens of Japanese extraction after Pearl Harbor, or prevent Senator McCarthy's short reign of terror. These are indeed conspicuous failures in the Supreme Court's long and on the whole creditable record. But it is absurd to think that internment or McCarthyism would not have occurred if America had had no Bill of Rights at all.

Some lawyers worry, however, that judges really could make things worse if the Convention were incorporated, because judges could then stand in the way of a Labour government's reforms by declaring novel social regulations invalid. They cite the decisions of the Supreme Court in the early 1930s which held important parts of Franklin Roosevelt's social legislation unconstitutional, until the 'Nine Old Men' of that Court gave way, by death and retirement, to new appointments. But a careful reading of the European Convention should reassure those who are worried by the analogy. The Convention was adopted by governments several of which had already embarked on welfare-state programmes. It contains a specific guarantee of the right to form and join trades unions, and no provision that any judge, no matter how conserva-

Interesting

49

tive, could use to strike down legislation a responsible Labour government would sponsor.

The Supreme Court in its most conservative period cited the Fifth Amendment, which provides that Congress may not deprive anyone of liberty or property without due process, to hold progressive legislation unconstitutional. It held, for example, that a New York law limiting the number of hours bakers could be asked to work each week deprived both bakers and their employers of the 'liberty' of contract. That use of the due process clause was legally indefensible, as even the most conservative American lawyers now almost all agree. But in any case there is no comparable clause in the European Convention.

The first protocol does provide that no one shall be deprived of 'possessions' except in accordance with principles of international law, and that states must 'respect the right of parents to secure ... education and teaching in accordance with their own religious and philosophical convictions'. It has already been established, through decisions of the Strasbourg Court, that these provisions would not permit a British government to confiscate private property with no compensation, or to abolish independent schools. (Britain accepted an even clearer prohibition on abolishing independent schools when it ratified the International Covenant on Civil and Political Rights in 1976.) But the protocol

leaves ample room for social legislation any responsible government would wish to enact; it insists, for
example, that a state may 'control the use of property in accordance with the public interest', and
it does not oppose obvious measures that would
decrease the unfair advantages of private schooling.
The risk is therefore inconsequential that after
incorporation judges would be able to stop social
and economic changes a future government of the
left would actually want, and would otherwise be
permitted to make.

Would Judges Become Politicians?

THE LAST objection in my catalogue argues that
if judges had the power to set aside legislation
as unconstitutional, judicial appointments would
become undesirably political, and judges would
be thought politicians themselves. British judges
already make politically sensitive decisions: they
review the legality of executive actions, for example,
and interpret and apply trades union law. Opponents of incorporation argue that allowing judges

an explicit power to declare statutes of Parliament invalid would make their political role greater and more apparent, and therefore reduce confidence in the independence of the judiciary. They point to the political character of high judicial appointments in America, and they cite, in particular, the national debate and partisan contest over Reagan's nomination of Judge Robert Bork to the Supreme Court in 1987.

That nomination battle was most extraordinary even in America, and it was provoked by Reagan's decision to appoint a judge who had made himself a political figure already. Bork had for many years campaigned among right-wing groups for his own nomination, promising in articles and speeches that he would revolutionise constitutional law. He denounced, and suggested that he would vote to overrule, a great number of well-established Supreme Court decisions that Americans had come to think of as the core of civil rights and racial justice in the United States. When the Senate rejected his nomination, Reagan appointed Anthony Kennedy instead, and though Justice Kennedy's judicial record suggested he would be a conservative judge – his record since appointment has been extremely conservative – the Senate approved him with no difficulty or acrimony.

There are important differences between the way judicial appointments are made in Britain and the

United States, moreover, which weaken the analogy. Though judges in Britain are largely drawn from a much too narrow sector of the population, and judicial appointments have tended to favour more conventional and conservative lawyers, these appointments are not regarded as political in a narrow, political-party, sense. Appointments are made by the Lord Chancellor, after consultation with senior judges, on a basis that seems to reflect a reasonably plausible combination of a candidate's seniority, success at the bar and esteem in the profession. Appointments are not reviewed in Parliament, as they are in the United States Senate.

Would it be necessary or desirable to change this system of appointment if judges had the power to strike down parliamentary statutes? If so, would the necessary changes make the process of appointment too political? It is far from clear that it would be either necessary or wise to make judicial appointments subject to parliamentary approval. In the United States the Senate's power to refuse a presidential nomination is a very real one. The Senate is never wholly controlled by the President, who makes nominations, and it is often controlled by the opposite party, as it was when Bork was rejected. So the process acts as a genuine check on presidential power. If a British Prime Minister began to control judicial appointments behind the scenes, however, a parliamentary check would be only a rubber-stamp, because a Prime Minister with an adequate majority can generally have his or her way on almost anything.

It is true that a requirement of parliamentary approval would give the opposition a chance to examine a candidate's record and qualification, and to expose inadequacies or biases that might show the appointment to be a political or ideological one. But the same examination could be made at least as well in other ways. The public is already more aware than it used to be of the importance of a particular judge's judicial attitude and philosophy. The long *Sypcatcher* litigation, for example, made the names and careers of several judges familiar to journalists and to an important part of the public. If judges had the additional powers that incorporating the European Convention would give them, the public would have even more interest in who the judges were, and the media would have that incentive for examining the qualifications of controversial appointees. So would academic lawyers, public interest groups and professional committees. A government whose judicial appointments did not follow the established pattern of selecting among barristers with the highest professional qualifications could expect the public to notice and strongly to disapprove.

It would therefore seem unwise, if the European Convention were incorporated, immediately to alter the traditional British process of judicial selection, which has so far raised no question of partisan party influence or executive tampering. If suspicion did begin to arise about judicial appointments, Britain could adopt other techniques of monitoring. As a matter of routine, the American Bar Association and other non-political professional groups publish their ratings of the legal ability of nominees to important courts, and Senators pay great attention to these ratings. The ABA has refused to endorse as qualified only one Supreme Court nominee in recent years – Judge Bork – but it has discouraged other judicial nominations by giving candidates relatively low ratings. If necessary, a committee with similar functions could be constituted in Britain (or could constitute itself) consisting of the officers from time to time of professional associations, law school deans or heads of faculties, and representatives of public interest legal groups. Such a group could call attention not only to doubtful appointees, but to other lawyers well-qualified according to traditional tests who were being passed over.

It might now be said, however, that if judges had more power over legislation, the traditional methods and standards for choosing them should change to make the bench deliberately more representative of the diverse groups and cultures within the British community. That is, in some ways, an appealing suggestion. But I think it should be resisted, at least until it becomes clear that adequate diversity will not be produced by the changes in the legal profession that are already underway and that incorporation would accelerate. The British public's sense that judges are not politicians gives Britain an important advantage over many other nations in making constitutional rights work. That sense would be jeopardised by a system of appointment which treated judges as representatives of sections of the population, because any such system would suggest that constitutional law is only politics in a different place.

Conclusion

CONSTITUTIONAL POLITICAL events – whether these are formal like Magna Carta and the Glorious Revolution or informal like the New Deal in America – define a nation's character in symbolism that cannot be fully appreciated at the time. Margaret Thatcher's long government will have been a constitutional event for liberty, one way or another, whatever happens. If the country acquiesces in freedom's decline, if censorship and intimidation and surveillance and the curtailment of ancient liberties generate no outrage but only indifference, if a complacent establishment calms itself with the false comfort that things are 'not so bad' or 'have never been all that much better', then the country will have lost a heritage not easily regained.

If, on the other hand, her high-handedness galvanises the British into a new concern for their old rights, and that concern is recognised and symbolised in a new constitutional charter, then the Thatcher era will have produced a constitutional event of an entirely different and grander character. The public will have announced that its culture of liberty is too valuable to trade for convenience or economy or repose. Britain will have taken an important step back towards her old place at the frontiers of personal freedom.

About the Author

RONALD DWORKIN is Professor of Jurisprudence at Oxford and a professor of law at New York University. His books include *Taking Rights Seriously*, *A Matter of Principle* and *Law's Empire*.

CHATTO
*C*ounter*Blasts*

Also available in bookshops now:-

Forthcoming Chatto Counter*Blasts*

Other CounterBlasts (and Specials) will include Shirley Hazzard on Waldheim and the United Nations, Brenda Maddox on the Pope and birth control, and Stephen Fry on education.

If you want to join in the debate, and if you want to know more about **Counter*Blasts***, the writers and the issues, then write to:

Random Century Group, Freepost 5066, Dept MH, London SW1V 2YY